Assessment of Riparian-Wetland Conditions and Recommendations for Management

Pueblo Colorado Wash, Hubbell Trading Post National Historic Site, Arizona

Natural Resource Report NPS/NRPC/NRR—2010/213

Joel Wagner

National Park Service
Natural Resource Program Center
Water Resources Division
P.O. Box 25287
Denver, Colorado 80225

Richard Inglis

National Park Service
Natural Resource Program Center
Water Resources Division
1201 Oak Ridge Drive, Suite 250
Fort Collins, CO 80525

June 2010

U.S. Department of the Interior
National Park Service
Natural Resource Program Center
Fort Collins, Colorado

The National Park Service, Natural Resource Program Center publishes a range of reports that address natural resource topics of interest and applicability to a broad audience in the National Park Service and others in natural resource management, including scientists, conservation and environmental constituencies, and the public.

The Natural Resource Technical Report Series is used to disseminate results of scientific studies in the physical, biological, and social sciences for both the advancement of science and the achievement of the National Park Service mission. The series provides contributors with a forum for displaying comprehensive data that are often deleted from journals because of page limitations.

All manuscripts in the series receive the appropriate level of peer review to ensure that the information is scientifically credible, technically accurate, appropriately written for the intended audience, and designed and published in a professional manner. This report received formal peer review by subject-matter experts who were not directly involved in the collection, analysis, or reporting of the data, and whose background and expertise put them on par technically and scientifically with the authors of the information.

Views, statements, findings, conclusions, recommendations, and data in this report are those of the author(s) and do not necessarily reflect views and policies of the National Park Service, U.S. Department of the Interior. Mention of trade names or commercial products does not constitute endorsement or recommendation for use by the National Park Service.

This report is available from the Natural Resource Publications Management website (http://www.nature.nps.gov/publications/NRPM).

Please cite this publication as:

Wagner, J. I. and R. Inglis. 2010. Assessment of riparian-wetland conditions and recommendations for management: Pueblo Colorado Wash, Hubbell Trading Post National Historic Site, Arizona. Natural Resource Report NPS/NRPC/NRR—2010/213. National Park Service, Fort Collins, Colorado.

NPS 433/103717, June 2010

Contents

Figures

Appendix

Executive Summary

Pueblo Colorado Wash is an integral feature of the cultural landscape preserved at Hubbell Trading Post National Historic Site (HUTR). During the 1970s and 1980s, exotic shrubs (tamarisk and Russian olive) invaded the wash. By about 1990, these shrubs had formed dense thickets that crowded out native vegetation and created a fire hazard that threatened the park's invaluable cultural features. At about this same time, a deep gully formed in the wash, further diminishing its natural and cultural resource functions and values. By the late 1990s, these threats prompted some critical resource management actions. Exotic shrubs were removed and small in-channel structures were installed to encourage development of a more stable channel form. Cottonwoods and willows were planted and livestock were excluded to help establish a healthy, native riparian-wetland plant community.

In 2008, the park superintendent asked the NPS Water Resources Division (WRD) to assess the condition of the riparian-wetland system in response to these and other restoration and management activities. During June 24-26, 2008, WRD staff used the Bureau of Land Management's Proper Functioning Condition method to evaluate the condition of the riparian zone. The lower half of Pueblo Colorado Wash (downstream reach) was rated "Functional – At Risk" with an upward trend. This riparian segment was considered marginally functional in that it has many of the vegetation and hydrology characteristics of a properly functioning riparian system. However, factors such as lack of a diverse, soil-binding wetland plant community and excess sediment inputs from headcuts upstream placed this reach in the "At-Risk" category. The upstream reach was also rated "Functional – At Risk" with an upward trend. In addition to having the same risk factors as the downstream reach, this segment exhibited inadequate riparian-wetland vegetative cover to protect banks and dissipate energy during high flows. These persistent risk factors leave the entire wash vulnerable to future channel and floodplain destabilization and degradation in larger storms.

Based on this condition assessment, the superintendent asked WRD to provide recommendations for addressing the immediate risk factors. This report recommends planting six herbaceous wetland species and several woody species to increase native plant diversity and cover. This would enhance wildlife functions and values by increasing the variety of habitats available for feeding, nesting, and so on, and would increase site stability and functionality by having multiple native plant species stabilize the channel and banks.

Park management also asked for recommendations for longer-term riparian area management in Pueblo Colorado Wash. Specifically, the superintendent posed two sets of questions:

1. What should be the long-term goal(s) for the Pueblo Colorado Wash riparian area within HUTR? Can the wash support a self-sustaining wetland-riparian vegetation community?

2. What is required to meet these goals? At what point should we stop planting wetland-riparian vegetation, i.e., how do we know when we are done with the revegetation effort?

Detailed responses to these questions, and recommendations for management, are provided in this report. However, some of the questions can't be fully answered without additional data collection and analysis. The Southern Colorado Plateau I&M network (SCPN) is currently establishing a long-term program to monitor vegetation, channel morphology, and hydrologic conditions in Pueblo Colorado Wash. Prior to this site visit, WRD and SCPN staff met to discuss ongoing monitoring and to determine what additional information would be needed to address these questions. We decided to install a network of shallow observation wells in the wash during this site visit so we could monitor seasonal and inter-annual water table fluctuations. These data will be useful in determining if appropriate conditions exist to support a self-sustaining riparian-wetland plant community and in identifying appropriate areas for additional riparian-wetland vegetation plantings.

Acknowledgments

We thank park Superintendent Anne Worthington for her extraordinary efforts in coordinating the management, restoration and monitoring of the Pueblo Colorado Wash. The work described in this report was conducted at her request and with her able assistance. Steve Monroe, Ellen Soles, and Jodi Norris of the NPS Southern Colorado Plateau Inventory and Monitoring Network (SCPN) played a huge role in installing the water table observation wells described in this report. They are among the hardest working and professional people we've worked with in the NPS, and were also very enjoyable companions during our field work and dinners together. A Southwest Conservation Corps crew (including Adrian Dineyazhe and Marcello Roanhorse) and a crew of Navajo Nation interns helped with well installation. They worked hard, were fun to work with, and were very much appreciated!

Introduction

Pueblo Colorado Wash is an integral feature of the cultural landscape at Hubbell Trading Post National Historic Site (HUTR). The historic site is managed by the National Park Service and is located in northeastern Arizona, just west of the town of Ganado (Figure 1). During the 1970s and 1980s, the wash was invaded by exotic shrubs (tamarisk and Russian olive). By about 1990, these shrubs had formed thickets in the wash area that crowded out native vegetation and created a fire hazard threatening HUTR's invaluable cultural features. At about the same time as the exotic shrub invasion, a deep gully formed along the length of the wash within the park (Shaw et al. 2005). Factors contributing to the gully formation are complex and not fully understood, but likely include exotic shrub invasion, presence of an upstream dam that alters natural hydrology and sediment processes, climate cycles, grazing practices, and natural arroyo processes that can move sediment downstream in pulses through alternating episodes of channel filling and incision.

By the late 1990s, threats to the park's cultural resources by expanding tamarisk and Russian olive thickets and worsening erosion in Pueblo Colorado Wash led to some critical resource management decisions. Removal of exotic shrubs from the wash area began in the late 1990s. Once that process was underway, William (Bill) Zeedyk, a retired US Forest Service biologist and now an environmental consultant from Sandia, NM, supervised installation of small, in-channel structures made of locally available rock (and later wood and rock). These hand-built structures, which were designed to encourage formation of meanders in the bottom of the straight, incised channel, were evaluated in a 2000 WRD trip report (Inglis). The structures are built low in the channel to allow lower flows to cut the gully walls, while flood flows would overtop the structures, leaving them intact. The idea was to slow channel flow by providing a wider floodplain, which would encourage deposition of sediment, raise the water table, provide sites for riparian vegetation to establish, and ultimately raise the elevation of the streambed and floodplain to reverse the incision process. Cottonwoods and willows were planted on the edges of the channel and on the adjacent terraces to help recovery of the riparian system, slow flood flows, accumulate sediment, and enhance wildlife values. Livestock grazing was excluded from the area to promote natural vegetation recovery and to allow new plantings to become established.

An upstream structure diverts flow into Ganado Lake, mostly during spring runoff (personal communication, Theresa Showa, Navajo Nation Department of Water Resources, July 2008). Sediment is trapped in a settling basin near the diversion structure and is flushed periodically back into the wash. This dam was renovated in the mid-1990s, and came back into use in 1998. Some irrigation releases are sent down Pueblo Colorado Wash; however, it is unknown how frequently this flow reaches HUTR.

Figure 2 shows a 1997 and 2007 photo pair of Pueblo Colorado Wash. The 1997 photo shows a straight channel undergoing active incision (note vertical, unvegetated banks, unvegetated channel bottom, and large rock/debris that was either transported to this location or exposed by high velocity flows). By 2007, after management actions were taken, the channel has aggraded significantly, the banks have flattened, and native riparian and wetland vegetation cover is increasing in the channel and on the floodplain. One of Bill Zeedyk's channel structures can be seen in the 2007 photo. Figure 3 shows a 1997 and 2010 photo pair of the wash, illustrating the response of the channel to these management actions farther downstream.

1

Riparian vegetation, channel morphology, and hydrologic conditions of Pueblo Colorado Wash were monitored by two investigators from 1998 through 2004 (Baker 2005; Zeedyk 2004). Zeedyk established and surveyed five cross-sections across the wash, creating a baseline for monitoring changes in channel and floodplain morphology. He also installed two water table monitoring wells. Even though these wells were measured infrequently and their spatial coverage of the wash is limited, they provide data describing a significant change (rise of greater than 2 meters) in riparian area ground water levels over a 10 year period of time.

During a brief site visit by WRD staff (Wagner) in summer 2007, park superintendent Anne Worthington explained that the Southern Colorado Plateau I&M network (SCPN) is establishing a long-term program in Pueblo Colorado Wash to monitor vegetation, channel morphology, and hydrologic conditions. This program is incorporating Zeedyk's cross-sections and wells into a more comprehensive monitoring system. At that time, we discussed the ongoing riparian-wetland revegetation work in the wash area and formulated two related sets of questions:

1) What should be the long-term goal(s) for the Pueblo Colorado Wash riparian area within HUTR? Can the wash support a self-sustaining wetland-riparian vegetation community?

2) What is required to meet these goals? At what point should the park stop planting wetland-riparian vegetation?

Anne submitted a 2008 technical assistance request to the Natural Resource Program Center for help with these complex questions. In February 2008, Rick Inglis, Joel Wagner, and Steve Monroe met to discuss ongoing monitoring in Pueblo Colorado Wash by the SCPN and to determine what additional information would be needed to address these questions. We decided to install a network of shallow observation wells in the wash so we could monitor seasonal and interannual water table fluctuations. These data would be useful in determining if appropriate conditions exist to support a self-sustaining riparian-wetland plant community and to identify appropriate areas for additional riparian-wetland vegetation plantings, if needed. We also decided to evaluate the current condition of the riparian system using the Bureau of Land Management's process for assessing the "Proper Functioning Condition" of riparian areas (USDI, 1998). This rapid assessment method involves evaluation of 17 hydrology, vegetation, and stream morphology factors to determine if a riparian system is in Proper Functioning Condition (PFC). It can also be used to identify characteristics of nonfunctional riparian systems that need to be addressed to move a site toward PFC.

On June 24-26, 2008 we worked with SCPN and park staff, a Southwest Conservation Corps crew, and a crew of Navajo Nation interns to complete the well installations. During this same time period we performed the riparian condition assessments.

Monitoring Well Network Installation

We installed a total of 11 shallow observation wells along the Pueblo Colorado Wash floodplain. A 12th well, installed by a contractor for the Bureau of Indian Affairs in September 2007, was incorporated into the monitoring system as well #10A. The wells were located along four transects that had been established previously by SCPN to monitor channel cross sections. These transects are oriented perpendicular to the channel and are spaced roughly evenly along the length of the wash within the HUTR boundary (transects 2, 4, 7, and 10 in Figure 4). Each transect is composed of three wells, with two on the south bank and one on the north bank. We had planned to place two wells on each side of the stream (total of four per transect), but in all cases the potential riparian area was relatively wide on the south side of the channel and very narrow (approx. 10-15 feet wide) on the north side. We felt that a single well on the narrow north floodplain at each transect was sufficient to evaluate water table fluctuations in those areas. Wells were labeled with the transect # and A-C from south to north, and are shown in Figure 4.

Wells were installed by hand using a 3.5 inch diameter bucket auger with 4 foot extensions. Holes were augered to approximately 4-5 feet below the top of the water table at each location. Since this was a relatively dry time of year (between spring snowmelt/rains and the monsoon season), we felt this depth was sufficient to measure March-October water levels, except perhaps in significant droughts. A well log was created for each installation to document soil types and characteristics encountered. Once each hole was augered to the appropriate depth, a well casing was quickly inserted and pushed to the maximum depth possible.

Each well casing was constructed using a 5-foot section of pre-slotted (0.02 in.), 2-inch diameter Schedule 40 PVC pipe. Unslotted 2-inch PVC riser pipe was attached to the top of the slotted section to achieve the necessary length for each well. A PVC cap was placed on the bottom of the casing to prevent sand from entering as it was inserted into the augered hole. Small holes were drilled in these end caps to allow water to drain out of them as water tables fall below the bottoms of the wells. The annular space around each slotted section of pipe was backfilled with commercial coarse filter sand, and river sand was used to backfill the rest of the space to within approximately two feet of the ground surface. Bentonite was then placed in the annular space to within about 6-12 inches of the surface, and concrete was then poured to bring the annular space up to the ground surface. A notch was made at the top of each well, which will serve as a permanent measuring point. The tops of the wells (at the measuring points) and ground surface elevations were surveyed to a common datum with a GPS and a total station. SCPN will provide these elevations at a later date.

We trained Adrian Dineyazhe and Marcello Roanhorse in operation and maintenance of an electronic tape measure that they will use to measure depths to the water table. Wells will be monitored every week during the growing season. They will record the data on the datasheets provided and will fax them to the Water Resources Division for entry in an Excel spreadsheet. The data will be graphed, checked for consistency, and forwarded regularly to SCPN staff and the park. SCPN staff will periodically monitor the well network and check the condition of the wells when they need to service continuous recording equipment or collect other monitoring data at HUTR. We recommend monitoring for at least two full growing seasons (March – October), and longer if possible. WRD and SCPN staff will work together to analyze the hydrologic data and will make recommendations regarding future plantings and the ability of the system to support a self-regenerating woody riparian plant community.

Functional Condition of the Riparian-Wetland System

We used BLM's process for assessing "Proper Functioning Condition" of riparian areas (USDI 1998) to evaluate the functional condition of the Pueblo Colorado Wash riparian zone. Possible riparian condition ratings include "Proper Functioning Condition," "Functional At-Risk" or "Nonfunctional" (see definitions below). The proper functioning condition of a riparian area refers to the stability of the physical system, which in turn is dictated by the interaction of geology, soil, water, and vegetation. A riparian area in PFC is in dynamic equilibrium with its streamflow forces and channel processes. The system adjusts to handle larger runoff events with limited change in channel characteristics and associated riparian-wetland plant communities. Because of this resiliency, riparian areas in PFC can maintain aquatic habitat, water quality enhancement, and other important ecosystem functions, even after larger storms. In contrast, nonfunctional systems in the same storms might exhibit excessive erosion and sediment loading, loss of aquatic and wetland habitat, and so on.

Based on assessment of 17 hydrologic, vegetation, and geomorphology elements of the riparian area, the team assigns one of the following three functionality ratings to a site:

Proper Functioning Condition: Streams and associated riparian areas are functioning properly when adequate vegetation, landform, or large woody debris is present to:

1. Dissipate stream energy associated with high water flows, thereby reducing erosion and improving water quality;
2. filter sediment, capture bedload, and aid floodplain development;
3. improve floodwater retention and groundwater recharge;
4. develop root masses that stabilize stream banks against cutting action;
5. develop diverse ponding and channel characteristics to provide habitat and the water depths, durations, temperature regimes, and substrates necessary for fish production, waterfowl breeding, and other uses; and
6. support greater biodiversity.

Functional-At Risk: These riparian areas are in functional condition, but an existing soil, water, vegetation, or related attribute makes them susceptible to degradation. For example, a stream reach may exhibit attributes of a properly functioning riparian system, but it may be poised to suffer severe erosion during a large storm in the future due to likely migration of a headcut or increased runoff associated with recent urbanization in the watershed. When this rating is assigned to a stream reach, then its "trend" toward or away from PFC is assessed.

Nonfunctional: These are riparian areas that clearly are not providing adequate vegetation, landform, or large woody debris to dissipate stream energy associated with high flows, and thus are not reducing erosion, improving water quality, sustaining desirable channel and riparian habitat characteristics, and so on as described in the PFC definition. The absence of certain physical attributes such as a floodplain where one should exist is an indicator of nonfunctioning conditions.

After examining site characteristics via aerial photography and on the ground, we divided Pueblo Colorado Wash into two assessment reaches. Width and vegetation cover of the riparian zones and sinuosity of the channel appeared to be different in the two reaches. The downstream reach extended from SCPN cross-section #1 to cross-section #6, and the upstream reach extended from cross-section #6 to cross-section #11 (Figure 4). Data sheets showing the results of the evaluations and detailed supporting notes are found in the Appendix.

Downstream Reach

This reach has shown dramatic improvements in channel and floodplain form since the riparian management activities discussed previously were implemented. The channel has aggraded from its former deeply-incised condition and the floodplain is now inundated in relatively frequent runoff events. Sinuosity is increasing somewhat, but this process is still ongoing. The channel is not yet considered "in-balance" with the sediment provided (it is actively aggrading and channel/floodplain form is still developing), but the direction is positive.

Riparian-wetland vegetation recovery has been dramatic since a site visit in 1997 (Figures 2 and 3). Cottonwood and willow plantings appear healthy, and coyote willow (*Salix exigua*) is spreading clonally and providing important stability to many upper streambank areas. Common three-square (*Schoenoplectus pungens*) has invaded much of the stream channel bottom and lower banks. These species are helping to slow velocities and dissipate stream energy, stabilize channel bottoms and banks, trap sediment, and perform other beneficial riparian functions. The system is clearly recovering from the non-functional condition observed here in the late 1990's to one that is more stable and developing more habitat values.

Several concerns were noted, however, with respect to riparian-wetland vegetation. We saw absolutely no evidence of cottonwood or willow recruitment from seed, even in the channel or on the lower banks. Cottonwood plantings over the last 10 years provide a scattered sapling age class, but it is unknown whether there will be establishment from seed in the future, or if plantings will always be necessary to provide new recruitment to replace aging and decadent trees. Similarly, willow plantings appeared vigorous, but only coyote willow has the capacity to spread clonally and stabilize additional streambank areas beyond the original plantings. If willows can't establish from seed along this reach, then more plantings will be needed to dissipate energy, provide bank stability and enhance riparian habitat values.

Another significant vegetation concern is the lack of species diversity in both the herbaceous wetland and woody riparian communities. There is a near monoculture of common three-square (*S. pungens*) in the channel and on the lower banks, with only a couple of small patches of hardstem bulrush *(Schoenoplectus acutus)*. Lack of herbaceous wetland plant diversity is a threat to channel stability and function. If *S. pungens* dies off due to disease, insect infestation, drought, or other reasons, there will be no other species present to contribute to these critical functions. Coyote willow (*Salix exigua*) is by far the predominant willow on the channel banks, but there are only very isolated shining willow (*Salix lucida*) and bluestem willow (*Salix irrorata*) plants present. This lack of diversity in upper channel bank species is a threat for the same reason as described above for the herbaceous plant community. If there is a dieback of coyote willow for any reason, then there will be no other species to stabilize the upper channel banks, trap sediment, dissipate energy, and provide the habitat functions offered by healthy willow communities.

The downstream reach was rated "Functional – At Risk" with an upward trend. It was considered marginally functional in that it has many of the vegetation and hydrology characteristics of a PFC system. In fact, it withstood large flood flows in fall 2007 (see photo in Figure 5), dissipating the energy of that event with apparently limited change in channel characteristics and associated riparian-wetland plant communities. But several factors clearly place the reach in the "At-Risk" category:

1. The effects of the diversion at Ganado Lake on downstream riparian areas (including HUTR) have not been analyzed, but thus far they have not prevented the riparian recovery observed to date. However, if farming increases in the area and there are greater demands for irrigation, more water may be diverted into Ganado Lake, including during the monsoon season. This could deprive downstream riparian areas (including HUTR) of water needed for establishment and maintenance of healthy and functional riparian-wetland vegetation.

2. Lack of diversity in herbaceous wetland plant species and willows creates risk that disease, drought, or insect damage could wipe out vegetation critical to riparian system recovery, stability and function.

3. If lack of cottonwood and willow reproduction from seed continues over the long term, then plantings will continue to be necessary to provide recruitment of new plants to replace those that are lost (see additional discussion in following section). Future managers at HUTR may not make planting in the riparian area as high a priority as the current and previous superintendent.

4. Active side channel headcuts upstream produce sediment that is handled now by the reach, but this sediment source will likely become a problem (excess sediment) in the future. The causes of the headcuts should be investigated and appropriate treatments should be implemented to stop excessive sediment delivery to the wash. We recommend that HUTR should request additional technical assistance from the NPS Natural Resource Program Center on this issue.

Continued positive developments including increasing native riparian-wetland vegetative cover, increasing channel sinuosity, and development of an appropriate channel/floodplain form (recovery from deep channel incision of the recent past) are reasons to identify the trend as "upward."

Upstream Reach

The hydrology, vegetation and geomorphology characteristics and PFC ratings of the upstream reach were very similar to the downstream reach. Therefore, rather than repeat all of the above discussion, we provide only a short summary here and point out any differences. The full PFC documentation and notes for both reaches are found in the Appendix.

The upstream reach was rated "Functional – At Risk" with an upward trend. The only difference in the rating factors between the two reaches was for factor #11 (Adequate riparian-wetland vegetative cover is present to protect banks and dissipate energy during high flows). In the upstream reach, we noticed some significant stretches of exposed (unvegetated) banks that are susceptible to erosion during bankfull or larger flows, and so recorded a "no" response. We recommend planting native wetland-riparian species on these unvegetated banks (see section below).

Regarding wetland-riparian vegetation, one notable difference was the addition of another herbaceous wetland plant species, saltgrass *(Distichlis spicata)*. This native, soil-stabilizing grass was observed along the upper streambanks in only a couple of isolated locations (e.g., on the north bank between transects 10 and 11). However, its presence indicates that it tolerates these site conditions, and it should be considered as a potential species for introduction to increase herbaceous wetland plant diversity and enhance channel bank stability.

A second notable vegetation difference was that cottonwoods were more numerous on the floodplain, presumably because of more plantings in this reach. However, as with the downstream reach, there was no evidence of establishment from seed.

The reasons for classifying this reach as "At-Risk" are the same as those listed above for the downstream reach, except we add a fifth factor of significant stretches of unvegetated channel banks that are vulnerable to excessive erosion.

Recommendations for Pueblo Colorado Wash Management Goals and the Revegetation Program

What should be the long-term goal(s) for the Pueblo Colorado Wash riparian area within HUTR? Can the wash support a self-sustaining wetland-riparian vegetation community?

There does not appear to be conclusive evidence regarding the "natural" or "pre-Anglo" channel form or riparian-wetland community in Pueblo Colorado Wash (Shaw et al. 2005). Therefore, park management must use its best judgment regarding the "desired condition" for Pueblo Colorado Wash, within the context of park purposes. We suggest that goals or desired conditions should include: 1) establish and maintain a riparian system that is in proper functioning condition (as defined previously); and 2) maintain a self-sustaining (i.e., self-reproducing), diverse, native wetland-riparian plant community that provides site stability and increased wildlife habitat values.

We assessed the status of this first suggested goal using the BLM's process for assessing "Proper Functioning Condition" of riparian areas (USDI 1998), and found that both stream reaches within HUTR are rated "Functional – At Risk." Recommendations for improving vegetation community diversity and other recommendations provided in this report should help move Pueblo Colorado Wash further toward the goal of "Proper Functioning Condition" and the second goal of a diverse native wetland-riparian plant community that increases wildlife values. However, whether the woody riparian community being established here will be "self-sustaining" is an open question that needs further explanation.

Cottonwood and willow seeds are released in late spring or early summer. In order to germinate and become established, these wind-borne seeds must fall on moist, bare soil surfaces in areas where the water table remains relatively close to the surface. The seeds are only viable for a short period (~1-2 weeks), so the linkage between timing of seed dispersal and availability of moist, bare seed beds on the upper channel banks and floodplain by spring or early summer is critical. Monsoon season storms in mid-July or later may produce appropriate substrates, but the seeds are no longer available to land and germinate. (Tamarisk has several competitive advantages over native woody riparian species, including an ability to produce seed throughout most of the growing season. Therefore, it can establish after monsoon season storms when cottonwood and willow seeds are no longer available to compete.)

Once cottonwood and willow seeds germinate, it is critical that the water table does not drop more than about 6 mm/day. This is because in order to become established, the seedling taproots must be in constant contact with the water table, and therefore must grow fast enough to keep pace with the falling water level. As a result, cottonwoods and willows generally will not establish from seed where water tables fall more than about 1 meter below the ground surface during the summer. The well network that we installed during this trip, along with the water level recorders and the stream channel crest gage installed by SCPN will give us a good idea if the basic water table characteristics exist to support establishment from seed in the future. If possible, we also suggest monitoring the timing of willow and cottonwood "seed rain" in the spring and early summer so we can see how seed availability and water levels match up. This can be as simple as identifying a few female cottonwoods and willows on site and recording dates when significant seed release begins and ends. WRD can provide further information for doing this, upon request.

The fact that we saw no cottonwood or willow establishment from seed is of some concern, but it doesn't mean such establishment can't occur here. The interval for cottonwood establishment along free-flowing rivers averages about 10 years (Lytle and Merritt, 2004), but may be much longer in some watersheds. For example, a site with a rapidly falling water table may require a rare sequence of events for cottonwoods or willows to establish, such as an unusually rainy summer that sustains an abnormally high water table for an extended period. Since recovery of the Pueblo Colorado Wash channel incision and development of potential establishment sites only occurred in the last few years, it is too early to determine if establishment from seed will occur in the future to replace older, decadent trees.

Extensive and expanding cover of common three-square (*S. pungens*) in the channel bottom and on the lower banks indicates that sufficient moisture exists to support a self-sustaining herbaceous wetland plant community. The issue for this community at HUTR is more about the lack of diversity, which minimizes wildlife values (e.g., limited food sources and habitat types) and is a risk to site stability, as explained previously. Recommendations for increasing native plant diversity and cover are found in the following section.

What is required to meet these goals? At what point should the park stop planting wetland-riparian vegetation?

If the goal is to establish a riparian system that is in proper functioning condition and has a self-sustaining, diverse native wetland-riparian plant community with increased wildlife habitat values,

8

then we strongly support continued planting of native cottonwoods, willows, and herbaceous wetland plants in the wash.

For cottonwoods, recruitment from seed is not yet occurring, so the planting program provides substitute recruitment of new plants to replace dying trees. Cuttings from Rio Grande cottonwoods (*Populus deltoides ssp. wislizeni*) should be used. Since these trees are dioecious (individual trees are either male or female), it is critical to make sure that poles of both sexes are planted to assure seed sources into the future. Poles should be inserted to a depth of 2 feet below the lowest expected water table in the growing season. (This information will be available as soon as we can collect a season or two of water table data from the newly installed wells.) Pole plantings should be located about 1-3 feet above the elevation of the channel bank so root systems can avoid long-term inundation (this is also the likely elevation zone for establishment from seed). They can be planted at higher elevations to achieve a desired landscape appearance, but poles will need to be quite long to meet the planting depth described above.

Unfortunately, there is no formula to determine when the number of planted cottonwoods is sufficient, and there is probably no such thing as "too many." We suggest planting in irregular clusters on the floodplain and leaving open areas without cottonwoods to provide diversity in habitat structure. On-center distances of 4-5 ft (1 pole per 2-3 square yards) within the clusters or groves would be a reasonable goal. The 2007 photo in Figure 2 shows this approximate planting density, and also shows them planted at the appropriate elevation with respect to the channel bank. During our visit it appeared that the planting effort has been more focused on the upstream reach. If the water table data support it, we suggest more new plantings in the downstream reach as well.

For willows, the ultimate goal should be to establish them along nearly all upper channel bank and adjacent low overbank areas. We suggest planting cuttings with on center distances of 1-3 feet for shrubby willows such as coyote willow (*S. exigua*) and bluestem willow (*S. irrorata*), interspersing the species. Although shining willow *(Salix lucida)* is found on site and plants are healthy, this is may be a little low in elevation for that species (personal communication, Dr. David Cooper, Colorado State University, July 2008). We suggest also considering planting Goodding's willow (*Salix gooddingii*). Because this is a tree species, it should be planted much farther apart than the shrubby willow species, at the tops of the banks or in low overbank areas. Again, these are dioecious plants, so care should be taken to obtain cuttings from many different plants to assure a mix of males and females.

For the herbaceous wetland plant community, we recommend planting more appropriate native species to increase diversity. This would enhance wildlife functions and values by increasing the variety of habitats available for feeding, nesting, and so on, and would increase site stability and functionality by having multiple species stabilize the soil. Discussions with several qualified vegetation ecologists and botanists working in the region indicated that the following species should be considered for introduction in Pueblo Colorado Wash:

Mountain rush *(Juncus arcticus)* – reported to exist in comparable riparian areas in the region (personal communication, Daniela Roth, Navajo Nation Department of Fish and Wildlife)
Chairmaker's bulrush *(Schoenoplectus americanus)* - reported in previous vegetation studies at HUTR

Common spikerush *(Eleocharis palustris)* – "*Eleocharis sp.*" is on SCPN species list for HUTR
Nebraska sedge *(Carex nebrascensis)*
Scratchgrass *(Muhlenbergia asperifolia)* - reported present at HUTR in previous studies
Saltgrass *(Distichlis spicata)* - observed in a few patches in the upstream reach at HUTR

All of these species are reported to occur in Apache County, AZ according to the USDA PLANTS database (http://plants.usda.gov/index.html) and would contribute to site stability, wildlife values, and ecosystem function. All can tolerate the slightly brackish conditions found at this site (specific conductance in the range of approximately 600 – 800 microsiemens/cm was measured in the channel by the USGS in 1998 - 2000). WRD can provide additional assistance with species selection, planting densities and locations, sources of plants, potential funding sources, and so on upon request.

At a basic level, the goals will be met when Pueblo Colorado Wash can be rated as being in Proper Functioning Condition. At that point, there will be an adequate channel form and at least the minimum native plant diversity, cover, and age class structure necessary to provide site stability and maintenance of wildlife habitat, even after large storms. Beyond that point, we would have to defer to the SCPN vegetation monitoring program to evaluate whether plant diversity is appropriate, and to wildlife experts to determine if additional habitat enhancements are appropriate and necessary.

Literature Cited

Baker, M. 2005. Analysis of Streamside Vegetation within Hubbell Trading Post Historic Site, Apache County, Arizona, Interim Report: Summary of 2004 Sampling. Report submitted to National Park Service, Hubbell Trading Post National Historic Site.

Lytle, D.A. and D.M. Merritt. 2004. Hydrologic Regimes and Riparian Forests: A Structured Population Model for Cottonwood. Ecology, Vol. 85, No. 9, pp. 2493-2503.

Shaw, H.G., P.M. Woodruff and W. Zeedyk. 2005. Natural History of a Small Place: An Ecological History of Pueblo Colorado Wash at Hubbell Trading Post National Historic Site, Ganado, Arizona. The Juniper Institute, Hillsboro, NM. 89 pp. (Final report submitted to HUTR)

U.S. Department of the Interior, Bureau of Land Management. 1998. Riparian Area Management: A User Guide to Assessing Proper Functioning Condition and the Supporting Science for Lotic Areas. TR 1737-15. BLM National Applied Resource Sciences Center. Denver, CO. 126 pp.

Zeedyk, W. 2004. Final Report: Geomorphological Monitoring and Instream Structure Installations. 72 pp., including appendix. (Final report submitted to HUTR)

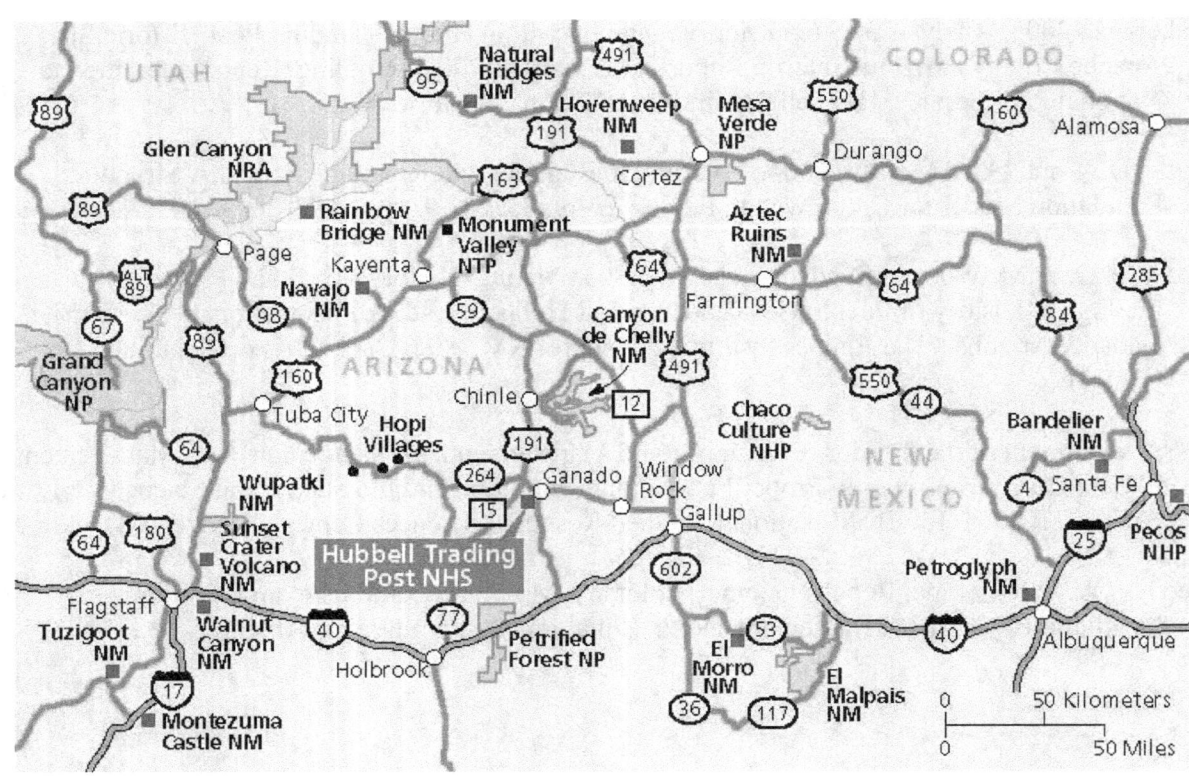

Figure 1. Location of Hubbell Trading Post National Historic Site

Figure 2. Photo pair of Pueblo Colorado Wash within HUTR, 1997 and 2007, looking west toward Hubbell Hill. Note in-channel deflection structure in 2007 photo (yellow arrow points to center of triangular structure). Photos by Joel Wagner, NPS.

Figure 3. Photo pair of Pueblo Colorado Wash within HUTR, 1997 and 2010, looking west toward Hubbell Hill. (Note failed rock gabion check dam in center of 1997 photo, since removed.) Photos by Joel Wagner, NPS.

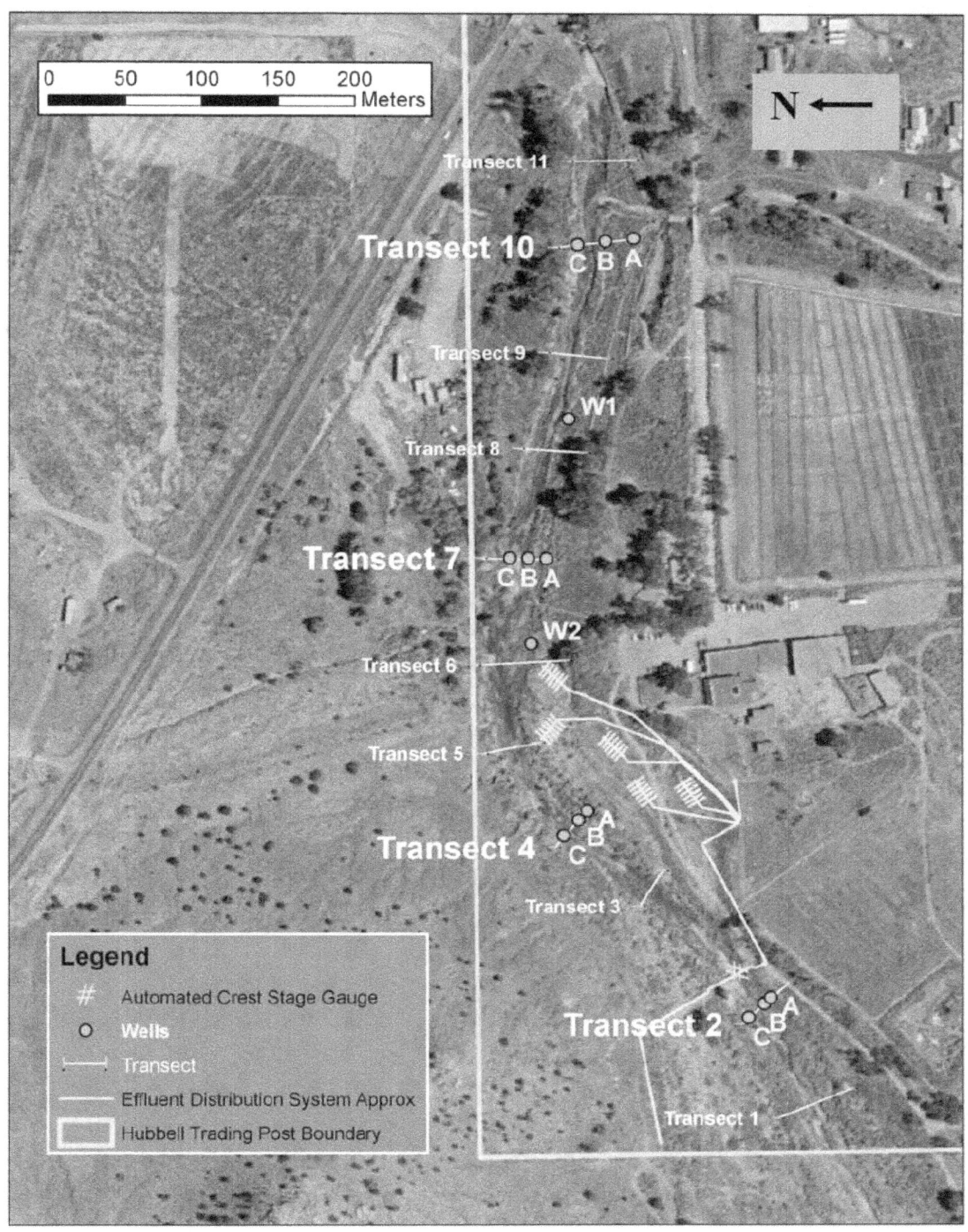

Figure 4. Locations of observation well transects installed June 24-26, 2008.

Figure 5. Pueblo Colorado Wash maintained its basic channel form and riparian-wetland vegetation community even after this large runoff event in fall 2007. Photo by Anne Worthington, NPS.

Appendix: PFC riparian system standard checklists and notes for downstream and upstream reaches of Pueblo Colorado Wash within HUTR

PFC Lotic (Riparian) Standard Checklist

Name of Riparian Area: __HUTR, Pueblo Colorado Wash near Ganado, AZ__
Date: __6-26-2008__   Segment/Reach ID: __Downstream reach, from SCPN cross-section #1 to cross-section #6__
Miles: __approx. 385 meters__   Acres:_____
ID Team Observers: __J. Wagner, R. Inglis_____

Yes	No	N/A	HYDROLOGY
X			1) Floodplain above bankfull is inundated in "relatively frequent" events
		X	2) Where beaver dams are present they are active and stable
	X		3) Sinuosity, width/depth ratio, and gradient are in balance with the landscape setting (i.e., landform, geology, and bioclimatic region)
X			4) Riparian-wetland area is widening or has achieved potential extent
X			5) Upland watershed is not contributing to riparian-wetland degradation

Yes	No	N/A	VEGETATION
	X		6) There is diverse age-class distribution of riparian-wetland vegetation (recruitment for maintenance/recovery)
	X		7) There is diverse composition of riparian-wetland vegetation for maintenance/recovery)
X			8) Species present indicate maintenance of riparian-wetland soil moisture characteristics
X			9) Streambank vegetation is comprised of those plants or plant communities that have root masses capable of withstanding high-streamflow events
X			10) Riparian-wetland plants exhibit high vigor
X			11) Adequate riparian-wetland vegetative cover is present to protect banks and dissipate energy during high flows
		X	12) Plant communities are an adequate source of coarse and/or large woody material (for maintenance/recovery)

Yes	No	N/A	EROSION/DEPOSITION
X			13) Floodplain and channel characteristics (i.e., rocks, overflow channels, coarse and/or large woody material) are adequate to dissipate energy
		X	14) Point bars are revegetating with riparian-wetland vegetation
	X		15) Lateral stream movement is associated with natural sinuosity
	X		16) System is vertically stable
	X		17) Stream is in balance with the water and sediment being supplied by the watershed (i.e., no excessive erosion or deposition)

(Revised 1999)

Remarks (numbers correspond to checklist items)

3. This system is responding to 10 years of management activities designed to aid recovery of the degraded riparian system of the late 1990s to one that is more stable and has higher habitat value. Actions have included exclusion of livestock, removal of tamarisk and Russian olive, planting of native willows and cottonwoods, and installation of in-channel rock and wood deflection structures. The channel and floodplain are actively aggrading and sinuosity is increasing. It is not yet considered "in-balance" but the direction is positive.

4. Common three-square (*Schoenoplectus pungens*) is growing nearly bank to bank in many areas. The riparian area is widening in these areas as the channel narrows.

5. The upland watershed may be aiding the improvement based on channel and floodplain aggradation and establishment of wetland vegetation (reach is not degrading). Side channel formation to the north in the upstream reach associated with concentrated highway runoff may become a threat (excess sediment delivery) at some point unless treated.

6. No evidence of cottonwood or willow recruitment from seed, even in the channel or on the lower banks. (*Salix exigua* is spreading clonally). Cottonwood plantings over the last 10 years provide a scattered sapling age class, but it is unknown whether there will be establishment from seed in the future, or if plantings will always be necessary to provide recruitment. Herbaceous riparian-wetland vegetation is essentially a monoculture of *Schoenoplectus pungens*. This species is spreading aggressively in the channel bottom and on lower banks. Both herbaceous and woody species are necessary for achieving PFC here.

7. Herbaceous species: a near monoculture of *Schoenoplectus pungens* in the channel and lower banks, with a couple of small patches of *Schoenoplectus acutus* in the channel thalweg. Lack of herbaceous wetland plant diversity is evident, and there is a threat to channel stability if *S. pungens* dies back.
   Woody species: coyote willow (*Salix exigua*) is by far the predominant willow on the channel banks and it is spreading clonally. Very isolated (though healthy) plants of shining willow (*Salix lucida*) and bluestem willow (*Salix irrorata*) present, likely from plantings. Scattered planted cottonwoods (*Populus sp.*) exist on the floodplain. Lack of diversity of upper channel bank species (willows) is a threat if there is a dieback of coyote willow.

16. Channel and floodplain actively aggrading and therefore not vertically stable. Episodes of mid-channel scour were reported by park staff this spring, but channel refilled soon afterwards.

17. Channel is actively aggrading.

Summary Determination

Functional Rating:		Trend for Functional – At Risk:	
Proper Functioning Condition	_____	Upward	__X__
Functional – At Risk	__X__	Downward	_____
Nonfunctional	_____	Not Apparent	_____
Unknown	_____		

Notes: Reach is considered functional in that it has many of the vegetation and hydrology characteristics of a PFC system. It withstood a very high flow event in fall 2007, dissipating the energy of that event with limited change in channel characteristics and associated riparian-wetland plant communities. But several factors place the reach in the "At-Risk" category:

1) An upstream dam diverts flow into Ganado Lake, mostly during spring runoff. Sediment is trapped in a settling basin near the diversion structure. Settling basin is flushed periodically, returning sediment to Pueblo Colorado Wash. Effects of these practices on downstream riparian areas (including HUTR) have not been analyzed, but may create risk. Also, if farming increases in the area and there are greater demands for irrigation, more water may be diverted into Ganado Lake, including during the monsoon season. This could deprive downstream riparian areas (including HUTR) of water needed for establishment and maintenance of stabilizing riparian-wetland vegetation.

2) Lack of diversity in herbaceous wetland plant species and willows creates risk that disease, drought, or insect damage could wipe out vegetation critical to riparian system stability and recovery.

3) If lack of cottonwood and willow reproduction from seed continues over the long term, then plantings will continue to be necessary to provide recruitment of new plants to replace those that are lost. Future managers at HUTR may not make planting in the riparian area as high a priority as the current and previous superintendent.

4) Active side channel headcuts upstream produce sediment that is handled now by the reach, but could become excessive.

Continued positive developments including increasing native riparian-wetland vegetative cover, increasing sinuosity, aggradation of the channel and floodplain formation (recovery from past deep channel incision) are reasons to identify the trend as upward.

Are factors contributing to unacceptable conditions outside the control of the manager?

    Yes   __X__

    No   _____

If yes, what are those factors?

    _X_ Flow regulations **(dam)** ___ Mining activities ___ Upstream channel conditions
    ___ Channelization ___ Road encroachment ___ Oil field water discharge
    ___ Augmented flows _X_ Other (specify) **active headcutting in side channels upstream**

PFC Lotic (Riparian) Standard Checklist

Name of Riparian Area: HUTR, Pueblo Colorado Wash near Ganado, AZ
Date: 6-26-2008   Segment/Reach ID: Upstream reach, from SCPN cross-section
#6 to cross-section #11
Miles: approx. 350 meters   Acres:
ID Team Observers: J. Wagner, R. Inglis

Yes	No	N/A	**HYDROLOGY**
X			1) Floodplain above bankfull is inundated in "relatively frequent" events
		X	2) Where beaver dams are present they are active and stable
	X		3) Sinuosity, width/depth ratio, and gradient are in balance with the landscape setting (i.e., landform, geology, and bioclimatic region)
X			4) Riparian-wetland area is widening or has achieved potential extent
X			5) Upland watershed is not contributing to riparian-wetland degradation

Yes	No	N/A	**VEGETATION**
	X		6) There is diverse age-class distribution of riparian-wetland vegetation (recruitment for maintenance/recovery)
	X		7) There is diverse composition of riparian-wetland vegetation for maintenance/recovery)
X			8) Species present indicate maintenance of riparian-wetland soil moisture characteristics
X			9) Streambank vegetation is comprised of those plants or plant communities that have root masses capable of withstanding high-streamflow events
X			10) Riparian-wetland plants exhibit high vigor
	X		11) Adequate riparian-wetland vegetative cover is present to protect banks and dissipate energy during high flows
		X	12) Plant communities are an adequate source of coarse and/or large woody material (for maintenance/recovery)

Yes	No	N/A	**EROSION/DEPOSITION**
X			13) Floodplain and channel characteristics (i.e., rocks, overflow channels, coarse and/or large woody material) are adequate to dissipate energy
		X	14) Point bars are revegetating with riparian-wetland vegetation
	X		15) Lateral stream movement is associated with natural sinuosity
	X		16) System is vertically stable
	X		17) Stream is in balance with the water and sediment being supplied by the watershed (i.e., no excessive erosion or deposition)

(Revised 1999)

Remarks (numbers correspond to checklist items)

3. This system is responding to 10 years of management activities designed to aid recovery of the degraded riparian system of the late 1990s to one that is more stable and has higher habitat value. Actions have included exclusion of livestock, removal of tamarisk and Russian olive, planting of native willows and cottonwoods, and installation of in-channel rock and wood deflection structures. The channel and floodplain are actively aggrading and sinuosity is increasing. It is not yet considered "in-balance" but the direction is positive.

4. Common three-square *(Schoenoplectus pungens)* is growing nearly bank to bank in many areas. The riparian area is widening in these areas as the channel narrows.

5. The upland watershed may be aiding the recovery based on channel and floodplain aggradation and establishment of wetland vegetation (reach is not degrading). Side channel formation to the north associated with concentrated highway runoff may become a threat (excess sediment delivery) at some point unless treated.

6. No evidence of cottonwood or willow recruitment from seed, even in the channel or on the lower banks. (*Salix exigua* is spreading aggressively vegetatively). Cottonwood plantings over the last 10 years provide a significant sapling age class, but it is unknown whether there will be establishment from seed in the future, or if plantings will always be necessary to provide recruitment. Herbaceous riparian-wetland vegetation is essentially a monoculture of *Schoenoplectus pungens.* This species is spreading aggressively in the channel bottom and on lower banks. Both herbaceous and woody species are necessary for achieving PFC here.

7. Herbaceous species: a near monoculture of *Schoenoplectus pungens* in the channel and lower banks, with a couple of small patches of *Schoenoplectus acutus* in the channel thalweg. Lack of herbaceous wetland plant diversity is evident, and there is a threat to channel stability if *S. pungens* dies back.
    Woody species: coyote willow *(Salix exigua)* is by far the predominant willow on the channel banks and it is spreading clonally. Very isolated (though healthy) plants of shining willow *(Salix lucida)* and bluestem willow *(Salix irrorata)* present, likely from plantings. Good numbers of planted cottonwoods *(Populus sp.)* exist on the floodplain. Lack of diversity of upper channel bank woody species (willows) is a threat if there is a dieback of coyote willow.

11. Some stretches of exposed (unvegetated) banks remain in portions of this reach.

14. Minor development of point bars but still in transition.

15. Some meanders forming but not stabilized and not yet affecting overall sinuosity/channel form.

16. Channel and floodplain actively aggrading and therefore not vertically stable. Episodes of mid-channel scour were reported by park staff this spring, but channel refilled soon afterwards.

17. Channel is actively aggrading.

Summary Determination

Functional Rating:		Trend for Functional – At Risk:	
Proper Functioning Condition	_____	Upward	X
Functional – At Risk	X	Downward	_____
Nonfunctional	_____	Not Apparent	_____
Unknown	_____		

Notes: Reach is considered functional in that it has many of the vegetation and hydrology characteristics of a PFC system. It withstood a very high flow event in fall 2007, dissipating the energy of that event with limited change in channel characteristics and associated riparian-wetland plant communities. But several factors place the reach in the "At-Risk" category:

1) An upstream dam diverts flow into Ganado Lake, mostly during spring runoff. Sediment is trapped in a settling basin near the diversion structure. Settling basin is flushed periodically, returning sediment to Pueblo Colorado Wash. Effects of these practices on downstream riparian areas (including HUTR) have not been analyzed, but may create risk. Also, if farming increases in the area and there are greater demands for irrigation, more water may be diverted into Ganado Lake, including during the monsoon season. This could deprive downstream riparian areas (including HUTR) of water needed for establishment and maintenance of stabilizing riparian-wetland vegetation.
2) Lack of diversity in herbaceous wetland plant species and willows creates risk that disease, drought, or insect damage could wipe out vegetation critical to riparian system stability and recovery;
3) If lack of cottonwood and willow reproduction from seed continues over the long term, then plantings will continue to be necessary to provide recruitment of new plants to replace those that are lost. Future managers at HUTR may not make planting in the riparian area as high a priority as the current and previous superintendent.
4) Active side channel headcuts upstream produce sediment that is handled now by the reach, but could become excessive.
5) Some stretches of exposed (unvegetated) banks remain in portions of this reach, leaving them vulnerable to excessive erosion.

Continued positive developments including increasing native riparian-wetland vegetative cover, increasing sinuosity, aggradation of the channel and floodplain formation (recovery from past deep channel incision) are reasons to identify the trend as upward.

Are factors contributing to unacceptable conditions outside the control of the manager?

Yes   _X_

No   ____

If yes, what are those factors?

_X_ Flow regulations **(dam)**   ___ Mining activities   ___ Upstream channel conditions
___ Channelization   ___ Road encroachment   ___ Oil field water discharge
___ Augmented flows   _X_ Other (specify) **active headcutting in side channels**

NPS 433/103717, June 2010